Of all the animals in the North American wilderness, none commands such fear, awe, and interest as the bear.

Stephen Herrerro
Bear Attacks, 1985

HAPPY HOLIDAYS

It had been a bitter cold and snowy winter, and everyone was anxiously awaiting the arrival of spring. At the annual holiday office party, you and your friends chatted about the best way to enjoy the approaching spring weather. One person, the leader of a local scout troop, proposed a camping trip. Although the rest of the group had little or no outdoor experience, the idea sounded intriguing. Another person mentioned an article she had read in National Geographic about the Appalachian Trail, a 2,144-mile footpath over the summits of mountains from Georgia to Maine. The Great Smoky Mountains National Park in North Carolina was noted as one of the most beautiful sections.

"We're all going to be in Raleigh, North Carolina this May for our work team retreat. How about a few days of backpacking when the meeting is over?" she suggested.

The Scout Leader, a small, wiry man, said it wouldn't be an easy trip, but he expressed confidence that everyone in the group could handle it. Without much more thought everyone agreed on a three-day trip to the Smokies in the spring.

THE TRAIL HEAD

Two days ago, May 13th, your group of 6 piled into a rented minivan after a successful meeting and headed to the base of the Smokies — Fontana Dam, North Carolina. The Scout Leader had assumed the responsibility for renting equipment from a local outfitter, putting the gear together for each person and purchasing food for the outing.

That night was spent at the trail head in the Fontana Dam Shelter, nicknamed the "Hilton" by local hikers. The wooden shelter, built in 1980 by the Tennessee Valley Authority, was a beautifully constructed, open-air hut with great views over the reservoir. The outside temperature was a comfortable 73° as the group enjoyed its first camp meal of baked beans and hot dogs cooked over the campfire. Everyone turned in early, excited about the next day of hiking.

SPRINGTIME IN THE SMOKIES

Yesterday morning your alarm clock was the melodious sound of the whippoorwill and chuck-will's-widow calling before dawn. As the sun edged over the mountains, you were greeted by a cloudless, pale-blue sky. After a breakfast of instant oatmeal, the packs were loaded and sturdy leather hiking boots were laced up. A Back Country Pass was completed at the self-registration station before you started out. You listed information about the size of your group and your group's intended destination for each day: Mollies Ridge Shelter on the first day and Cades Cove, where you were to be picked up, on the second day.

With backpacks on, your group headed across the dam, following the painted white blazes that mark the Appalachian Trail. After crossing to the other side of the dam, you followed another hard-surfaced road to the right for a half-mile and then entered the forest at an intersection with an abandoned dirt road.

THE APPALACHIAN TRAIL

The well-marked, two-foot-wide trail ascended steeply, switching back periodically. It wasn't an easy climb for your group, but the magnificence of the forest viewed from underneath the canopy of broad-leaf, hardwood trees was captivating. The Scout Leader guided your group up the trail, following the signs north, and pushing on at a good pace. The group's enthusiasm was tempered by the difficulty of the hike, but no complaints were heard — it was invigorating to be in the great outdoors.

MOLLIES RIDGE SHELTER

By the time your group reached Mollies Ridge Shelter at 4:30 pm, everyone was tired and sweaty. The three-sided, open-front lean-to here was much more primitive than the "Hilton." The walls were built from field stones, and the open side was secured with a chain-link fence. It was dark and cool inside the shelter. Most of the space inside was taken up by a wooden sleeping platform. You all dropped your gear in the shelter and sat down to rest. Eating a hot meal and changing into warm, dry clothes lifted everyone's spirits. Conversation ended early — the group was completely worn out.

Everyone awakened late at 10:00 am this morning. The sun barely shone through the cloudy skies; more ominous clouds edged along the horizon. You ate a quick breakfast, then packed up your gear and began your hike out.

The sky grew darker and a light rain began to fall as you arrived two hours later at Russell Field Shelter. You eagerly ate a hot lunch of macaroni and cheese. By the time you had packed your gear again the rain had stopped, but a thick, tree-top fog had rolled in.

"We'd better get going," the Scout Leader instructed. "It's about 5 miles to Cades Cove." From the shelter the group headed north down the well-worn Russell Field Trail, leaving the Appalachian Trail behind.

AN UNWELCOME SURPRISE

A couple of miles into the hike the Scout Leader suddenly stopped. "Anyone like fresh blue-berries?" he asked, pointing to the fruit-laden bushes lining the trail. Packs were quickly dropped as you each picked and ate your way in different directions along the trail.

"There's tons of berries over here," one person called excitedly. "Hey, look what I found!" A small black bear cub tumbled from the bushes.

"Get away from the cub! The mother may be nearby!" yelled the Scout Leader, as he rushed toward the hiker. Before anyone could move, a large black bear exploded out of the under-brush, knocking down the Scout Leader. Everyone was frozen with fear.

"Climb a tree!" one person yelled. A couple of you turned and ran. The Scout Leader curled up to play dead as the bear repeatedly clawed at him with a heavy paw. Some group members stood their ground, screaming and throwing anything they could find at the bear. In a flash it was over. The group finally frightened the bear away. The mother bear with cubs in tow dis-appeared up the trail toward Cades Cove.

Now, cautiously, everyone has moved to the Scout Leader's side. He is lying on the ground unconscious, covered with pine needles, leaves, and dirt. He is bleeding steadily from deep lacerations on his chest, arms, and back from the bear's claws, but does not appear to have any broken bones.

The trip has turned into a disaster. Some of you are concerned that the Scout Leader is going into shock. All of you fear that he won't survive unless he reaches proper medical help within the next few hours.

"We have to get him help fast! There's got to be a helicopter medivac team at a hospital somewhere near here."

"They'll never find us with this fog. We've got to move him now!"

Now someone asks the unthinkable: "What if the bear returns?"

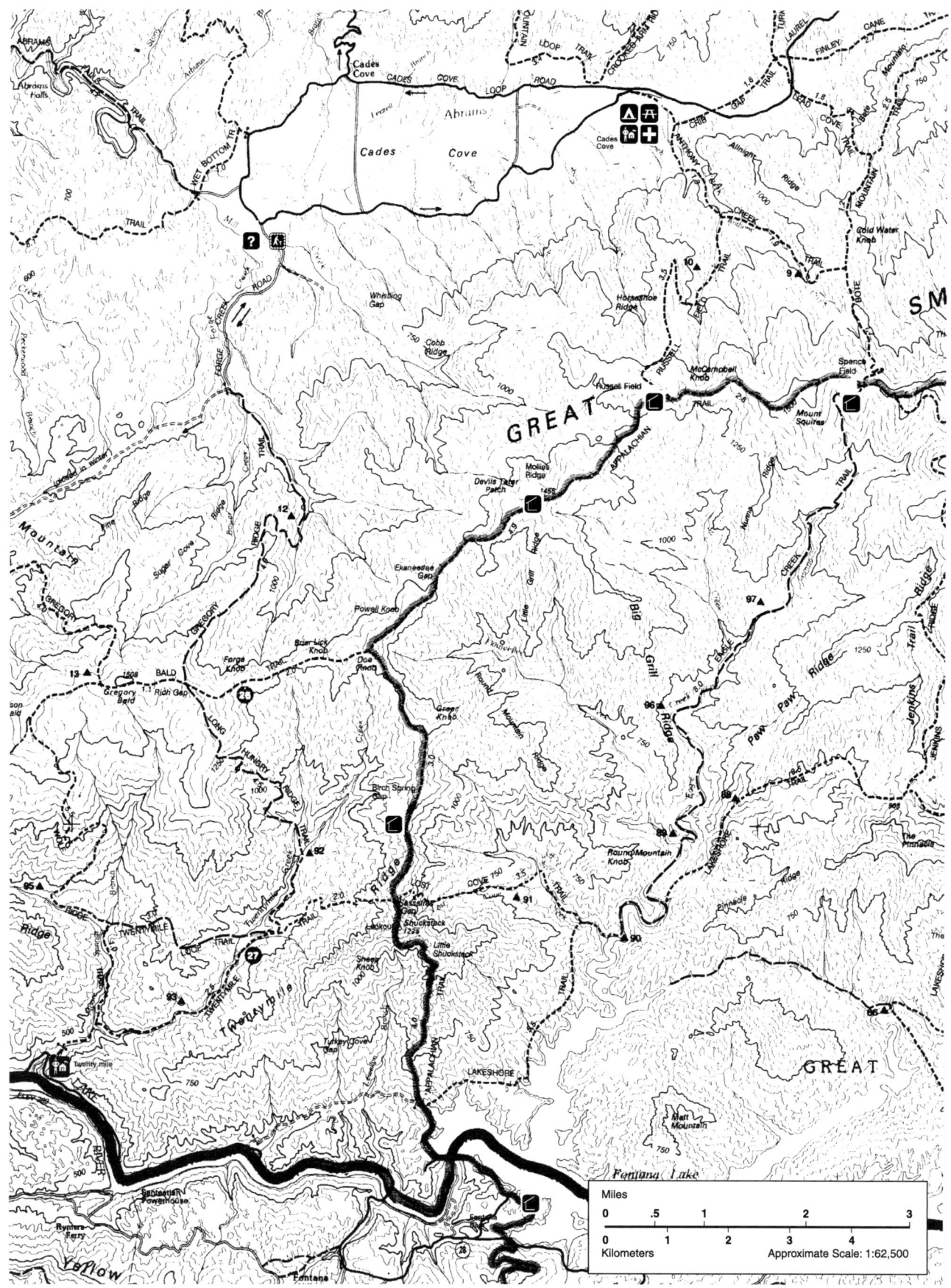

Reprinted with permission. Trails Illustrated Topo Maps, Evergreen, CO. Please note: the map has been slightly altered for the purposes of this exercise.

SCORING FORM — STRATEGY ALTERNATIVES

	A	B	C
Strategy Alternatives	**Individual Choice**	**Expert Points**	**Team Choice**
Alternative 1 Send some of the group members back to Russell Field Shelter for help while the others remain with the injured person and provide first aid.		18	
Alternative 2 Everyone stays with the Scout Leader, providing first aid and signaling for help while waiting to be rescued.		20	
Alternative 3 Send some of the group members to Cades Cove Ranger Station for help while the rest remain with the injured person and provide first aid.		15	
Alternative 4 Administer first aid to the Scout Leader, allowing him a short time to stabilize, and then evacuate him to Cades Cove Ranger Station.		0	
Alternative 5 Evacuate the Scout Leader immediately to Cades Cove Ranger Station.		10	
	Individual Subtotal		**Team Subtotal**

Scoring Directions

1. Expert points for each Alternative appear in Column B of the chart. Enter the points that match your Individual Choice into the Subtotals box below Column A. Enter the points for the Team Choice into the Subtotals box below Column C.

2. Transfer these Subtotals to the corresponding boxes of the Scoring Chart on the Backpack Items Form.

3. An Expert Ranking for the Backpack Items is recorded in Column C of that chart. For each item, calculate the difference between your Individual Ranking (Column A) and the Expert Ranking (Column C), no pluses or minuses. Place the differences in Column B. Add the difference scores in Column B and place the sum in the Subtotal box below.

4. Calculate the difference between the Team Ranking (Column E) and the Expert Ranking (Column C). Place the differences in Column D. Add the difference scores in Column D and place the sum in the Subtotal box below.

5. Transfer these Subtotals to the corresponding boxes of the Scoring Chart below. Add the Subtotals to obtain your Total Individual and Total Team Scores.

Black Bear

EXPERT CHOICE AND RATIONALE — STRATEGY ALTERNATIVES

Strategy Alternative 1: *Send some of the group members back to Russell Field Shelter for help while the others remain with the injured person and provide first aid*, is ranked fourth by the experts because it does not resolve the major issue of getting proper medical attention for the injured as quickly as possible. Valuable time will be lost sending some people back to a site where there are no medical facilities and perhaps no one even there who might be of some assistance.
(18 points)

Strategy Alternative 2: *Everyone stays with the Scout Leader, providing first aid and signaling for help while waiting to be rescued*, gives the Scout Leader the lowest chance for survival. With the dense fog there isn't much you can do to signal. Because no one will suspect your group is in trouble for a few days, help for the injured could be a long time in coming.
(20 points)

Strategy Alternative 3: *Send some of the group members to Cades Cove Ranger Station for help while the rest remain with the injured person and provide first aid*, is also ranked low by the experts. It will take too much time to get to the ranger station and back with any kind of help. Even if you called for a helicopter, the dense fog would make such a rescue nearly impossible. Valuable time would be lost that could have been used to carry the injured person to medical care.
(15 points)

Strategy Alternative 4: *Administer first aid to the Scout Leader, allowing him a short time to stabilize, and then evacuate him to Cades Cove Ranger Station*, is the best strategy for saving the Scout Leader's life because it is the quickest method of getting him to the required medical help. Although the group is not an experienced medical-evacuation team, the Cades Cove Ranger Station is only 3-4 miles away over moderate terrain, and the salvageable Backpack Items can supply the needed equipment to create a carrying device. The group has sufficient time to administer first aid, prepare the litter, and transport the Scout Leader to Cades Cove for proper medical care.
(0 points)

Strategy Alternative 5: *Evacuate the Scout Leader immediately to Cades Cove Ranger Station*, receives a lower ranking from the experts because it does not give the group time to provide first aid, assess the situation   adequately, or work out the details of a wilderness rescue plan, thereby increasing the risk of further injury to the Scout Leader and the other group members. It ranks higher than Alternatives 1, 2, or 3 because this strategy, although it does not allow any time for planning, could get the Scout Leader to medical help in the shortest time.
(10 points)

Black Bear

RESPONSE FORM — STRATEGY ALTERNATIVES

Strategy Alternatives	A Individual Choice		C Team Choice
Alternative 1 Send some of the group members back to Russell Field Shelter for help while the others remain with the injured person and provide first aid.			
Alternative 2 Everyone stays with the Scout Leader, providing first aid and signaling for help while waiting to be rescued.			
Alternative 3 Send some of the group members to Cades Cove Ranger Station for help while the rest remain with the injured person and provide first aid.			
Alternative 4 Administer first aid to the Scout Leader, allowing him a short time to stabilize, and then evacuate him to Cades Cove Ranger Station.			
Alternative 5 Evacuate the Scout Leader immediately to Cades Cove Ranger Station.			

Your Task Now

Your Individual Task

In the chart above are five Strategy Alternatives for your group to consider. The Backpack Items Response Form has a list of 10 items that have been salvaged from your backpacks. Other than car keys, pocket money, and a map of the trail (see a section of this map on page 4 of your Participant Guide), your group has no other possessions. On page 5 you will find some additional charts that may be helpful to you.

Your first task is to select the *single best* Strategy Alternative for *the Scout Leader's survival*. In Column A of the chart (Individual Choice), place an "X" in the box next to the Alternative you have chosen. You may wish to look over the Backpack Items before making your selection. Next, rank the Backpack Items in order of their importance to executing the Strategy Alternative you have selected. Rank the most important item "1," the second most important item "2," down to the least important item "10." Place your rankings in Column A (Individual Ranking) of the Backpack Items chart. Your facilitator will tell you how much time you have for this task.

Please read the additional instructions on the Backpack Items Response Form before you begin.

Black Bear

RESPONSE FORM — BACKPACK ITEMS

	A		E
Backpack Items	**Individual Ranking**		**Team Ranking**
Smith & Wesson .22 caliber automatic pistol; 8-shot capacity magazine; fully loaded			
Five 1-liter plastic water bottles with lids; empty			
Backpacker's gas stove; tank half full			
How to Stay Alive in the Woods by Bradford Angier; paperback			
Three external frame backpacks			
Oil-filled compass with rotating bezel and signaling mirror			
Five synthetic-filled, 30° sleeping bags			
Two 50' bundles of nylon parachute cord			
Two small tins of sardines			
Backpacker's first aid kit			

If you make an error, please do not erase. Your responses are being recorded on pressure-sensitive paper. Simply cross out your answer and write the new answer in the same space. When you are finished with the two tasks, please do not discuss the scenario or your responses. Hold this information for the team discussion that will follow. You may wish to read the information on pages 6–8 unless you have been directed otherwise by your facilitator.

The Team's Task

Having selected the best Strategy Alternative and ranked the 10 Backpack Items independently, your team is now ready to share its views and rankings. Remember that your team is the group in this situation. With your team select the one best Strategy Alternative for the Scout Leader's survival and place an "X" in Column C (Team Choice) to indicate the Option you have selected. Next, with your team rank the 10 Backpack Items, considering the Strategy Alternative you chose as a team. Place the team's ranking in Column E (Team Ranking) of the Backpack Items chart. Please do not change your individual rankings as a result of the team discussion. Your facilitator will tell you how much time you have for your discussion.

Black Bear

EXPERT RANKING AND RATIONALE — BACKPACK ITEMS

The ranking of the Backpack Items is based on the following priorities: providing first aid to the victim, constructing a carry litter, and carrying the Scout Leader to safety.

1. **Backpacker's first aid kit** — A simple backpacker's emergency first aid kit, though usually lacking supplies for every contingency, will contain items usable in this situation. Gauze bandages, adhesive tape, and antiseptic towelettes can be used to clean and cover the wound. Direct pressure should be applied to slow the bleeding.

2. **Five synthetic-filled, 30° sleeping bags** — A sleeping bag placed over the Scout Leader could make the difference between life or death. "If it's cold, the patient does not have the advantage you enjoy of being able to exercise to increase personal warmth. Great attention should be paid to keeping a patient warm" (Tilton, 1990, p. 25). Cool May weather in the Smokies combined with lost blood can greatly increase the victim's risk of shock.

3. **Three external frame backpacks** — The best evacuation litter can be constructed using three external backpack frames. The pack-frame litter is made by lashing the frames together end to end using rope or cord. It is then padded for the patient's comfort.

4. **Two 50' bundles of nylon parachute cord** — This thin, braided cord is essential for building a pack-frame litter and securing the victim. A combined length of 100 feet will be enough to fasten the backpack frames together and strap down the victim for transport.

5. **Five 1-liter plastic water bottles with lids; empty** — Evacuating an injured person from the woods is physically demanding work. Having a method of collecting and carrying fresh water is critical. One liter of water per person is a minimal requirement for preventing complete dehydration before reaching the ranger station.

6. **Two small tins of sardines** — It will be a few hours before the group reaches civilization. It is not likely that the group will die of starvation, but a little nourishment can help to keep everyone including the victim energized.

7. ***How to Stay Alive in the Woods* by Bradford Angier; paperback** — In this classic book Angier provides detailed information on finding sustenance, warmth, orientation, and safety in the wilderness. The chapter on first aid could be of use to the group but, for the most part, the book is written for persons who need to live in the woods for a period of time while waiting to be rescued. Most of the book will be of little use, as this group's best plan of action is evacuation.

8. **Oil-filled compass with rotating bezel and signaling mirror** — Without a compass effective travel through unmarked territory would be impossible. Fortunately, trails in the Smokies, especially the Appalachian Trail, are well marked. They are also well worn from use and are therefore easy to follow. If the group members were to become lost, the compass would become invaluable, but that situation is unlikely. Although improbable, would-be rescuers could be signaled with the attached mirror if the skies clear up and the sun shines.

9. **Smith & Wesson .22 caliber automatic pistol; 8-shot capacity magazine; fully loaded** — A high-powered rifle or pistol in the hands of an experienced shooter can stop an attacking bear. But a small caliber handgun like the .22, especially in the hands of a novice, could do more harm than good. In this situation the gun's value is low, partly because of its size, but mostly because the bear is unlikely to return.

10. **Backpacker's gas stove; tank half full** — This small backpacker's stove could be used to boil water for purification, to cook food, and even to provide warmth if the group were staying. For evacuation purposes it serves little or no use.

Black Bear

SCORING FORM — BACKPACK ITEMS

Backpack Items	A Individual Ranking	B Difference	C Expert Ranking	D Difference	E Team Ranking
Smith & Wesson .22 caliber automatic pistol; 8-shot capacity magazine; fully loaded			9		
Five 1-liter plastic water bottles with lids; empty			5		
Backpacker's gas stove; tank half full			10		
How to Stay Alive in the Woods by Bradford Angier; paperback			7		
Three external frame backpacks			3		
Oil-filled compass with rotating bezel and signaling mirror			8		
Five synthetic-filled, 30° sleeping bags			2		
Two 50' bundles of nylon parachute cord			4		
Two small tins of sardines			6		
Backpacker's first aid kit			1		

Individual Subtotal   Team Subtotal

Scoring Chart

	Individual Subtotals	Team Subtotals
Strategy Alternatives		
	+	+
Backpack Items		
	=	=
Totals		
	Individual	Team

Black Bear

CONVERSION CHARTS

LEGEND

Paved Road	————————
Light-Duty Road – Hard or Improved Surface	════════
Unimproved Road	═══ ═══
Unmaintained Trail	▬ ▬ ▬ ▬ ▬ ▬
Hiking Trail	▪ ▪ — ▪ ▪ — ▪ ▪ —
Horse and Hiking Trail	▬ ▬ ▬ ▬ ▬ ▬ ▬
Appalachian Trail	▬▬▬▬▬▬
Selected Trail	**48**
Nature Trail	🚶
Developed Campground	▲
Backcountry Campsite	21▲
Backcountry Shelter	◣
Picnic Area	⛩
Ranger Station	👫
First Aid Station	✚
Visitor Center	❓
One Way	→
Gate	•—•
Mileage between Intersections	*4.8*
Wooded Cover	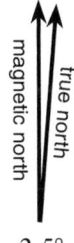
National Park Boundary	▬▬ ▪ ▬▬
Interstate Highway	⬭
US Highway	⬡
State or County Road	◯

CONVERSION TABLE

Meters	Feet
1	3.2808
2	6.5617
3	9.8425
4	13.1234
5	16.4042
6	19.6850
7	22.9659
8	26.2467
9	29.5276
10	32.8084

To convert meters to feet
multiply by 3.2808

To convert feet to meters
multiply by 0.3048

magnetic north   true north

2.5°
Mean Magnetic Declination

Contour Interval: 50 Meters

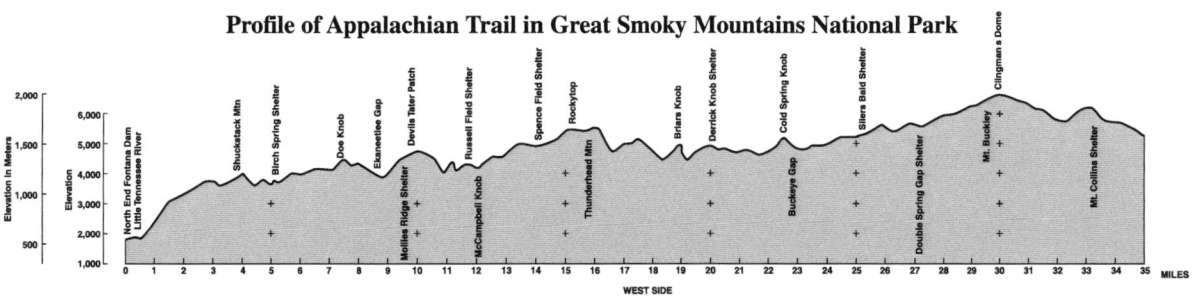

Profile of Appalachian Trail in Great Smoky Mountains National Park

A GUIDE FOR IMPROVING YOUR TEAM DISCUSSION

Black Bear has been designed to provide your team with the experience of making decisions under pressure, which usually occurs when there is a shortage of time or resources and the decision has important consequences. Although your team may not encounter life and death situations like a bear attack, there will be times when it must make important or critical decisions, when the time frame is too short and the available resources are inadequate.

There are many possible stumbling blocks to effective team decision making under pressure. They include the difficulty of sorting through massive information; relying on traditional ways of solving problems; becoming over-committed to an initial decision; pushing for unanimous decisions instead of applying rational thinking; and others.

The model in figure 1 suggests a decision-making process using team member behaviors that can be effective when a group is pressured to take quick action. The first part of the process involves gathering and generating as much information as possible. This information is then filtered through critical thinking before a decision is made. Decisions are continually reviewed to make sure that they are still the best possible decisions.

The seven team actions are identified in figure 1 and described on the next page. These actions should be used to the extent possible within the time constraints, rather than simply allowing one person to make the decision or following the course of least resistance.

Figure 1. Effective Team Decision-Making Process Model

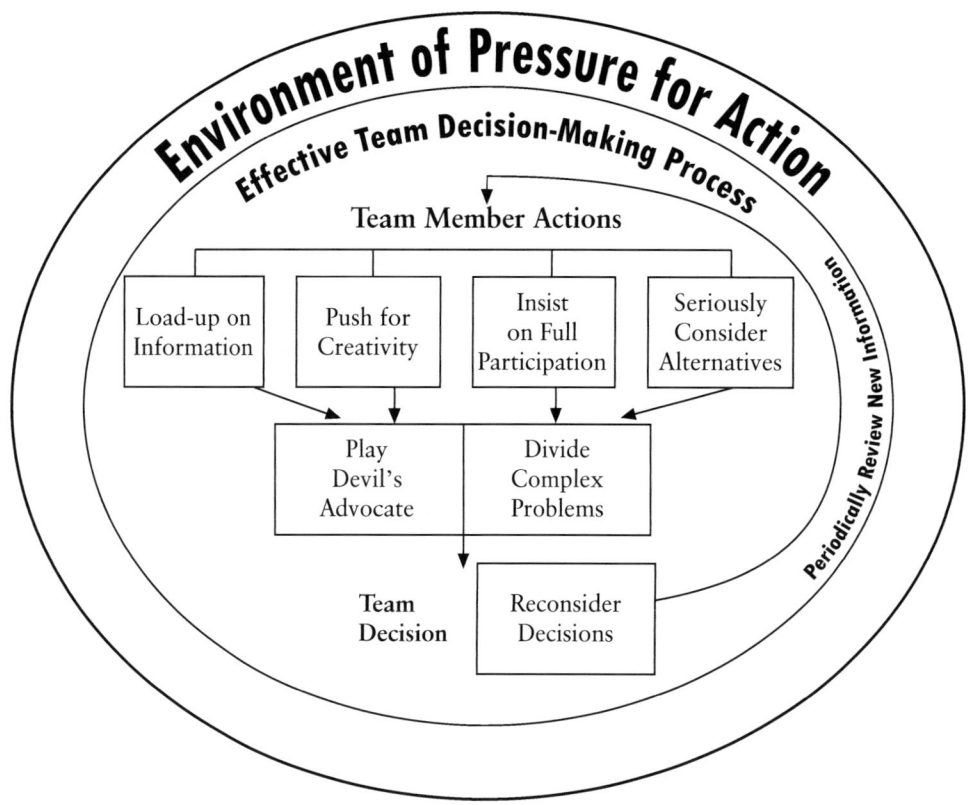

THE CHALLENGE OF DECISION MAKING UNDER PRESSURE

It is difficult to practice all the team member actions in the model, even under the best circumstances. Decision-making under pressure makes practicing these behaviors even more challenging. But in a high-pressure situation, use of good decision-making techniques becomes crucial. With practice, these seven actions can help you improve your team's ability to make effective decisions, regardless of stress and pressure.

Load-up on Information   *Obtain and actively listen to as much information as possible*
A key factor in successful decision making under pressure is the ability to obtain and share a wealth of information. Listening to several sources counteracts any particular biases one individual source may have.

Push for Creativity   *Look for new ways to view situations and solve problems*
New and innovative solutions should be generated rather than falling back on what has been done in the past. One method for generating new solutions is to split the group into subgroups and have each subgroup generate options.

Insist on Full Participation   *Make sure all team members are fully involved*
Ensuring full participation in decision making promotes commitment to the final decision. In addition, including as many perspectives as possible increases the likelihood that an effective decision will be made.

Seriously Consider Alternatives   *Allow sufficient time to discuss alternatives*
One of the stumbling blocks to effective decision making under pressure is the tendency to engage in groupthink — to seek group unanimity without a thorough discussion. One way to combat this problem is to insist on a discussion of alternative scenarios and solutions before a decision can be made.

Play Devil's Advocate   *Challenge assumptions and carefully evaluate ideas*
In high-pressure decision making, people's assumptions may go unchallenged in an effort to reach a quick decision. A devil's advocate takes responsibility for challenging assumptions and urges careful consideration of any suggestion offered. The ideal situation exists when each team member takes the responsibility for playing this role during a discussion.

Divide Complex Problems   *Separate major decisions into small, manageable ones*
One problem with decision making under pressure is that high-pressure situations can be quite complex. It helps to break down a major decision into smaller decisions. Handling a series of small decisions is less overwhelming than trying to tackle a complex decision all at once.

Reconsider Decisions   *Continually review decisions to make sure they are still the best*
Decisions should be reviewed periodically or in the light of new information. The need to evaluate a decision does not end once the decision is made. The team should not ignore new, relevant information simply because it has already agreed upon a decision.

7

SYNERGY

What is synergy? How do we achieve it?

Synergy is derived from the Greek word, *syn*, meaning together, and *energy*. Synergy is the special energy which is created when people work together effectively on a project or problem. This energy is usually stronger and more powerful than the energy created by individuals working alone. The secret to synergy is how people work together.   The model below illustrates how teams develop synergy.

The top pyramid represents the individual expertise, experience, knowledge, and skills that individuals in a group possess. The way in which a group taps into its individual resources is the key to building synergy. The second point of the triangle, problem solving, reflects the use of an organized system for approaching problems and developing solutions. If the group has a shared frame of reference for problem solving, the chances of reaching synergy are increased. The final point of the triangle represents the skillful use of interpersonal skills during discussion. The potential for a synergistic outcome is increased if the group possess the interpersonal skills necessary to communicate their ideas effectively.

Figure 2. A Model of Team Synergy

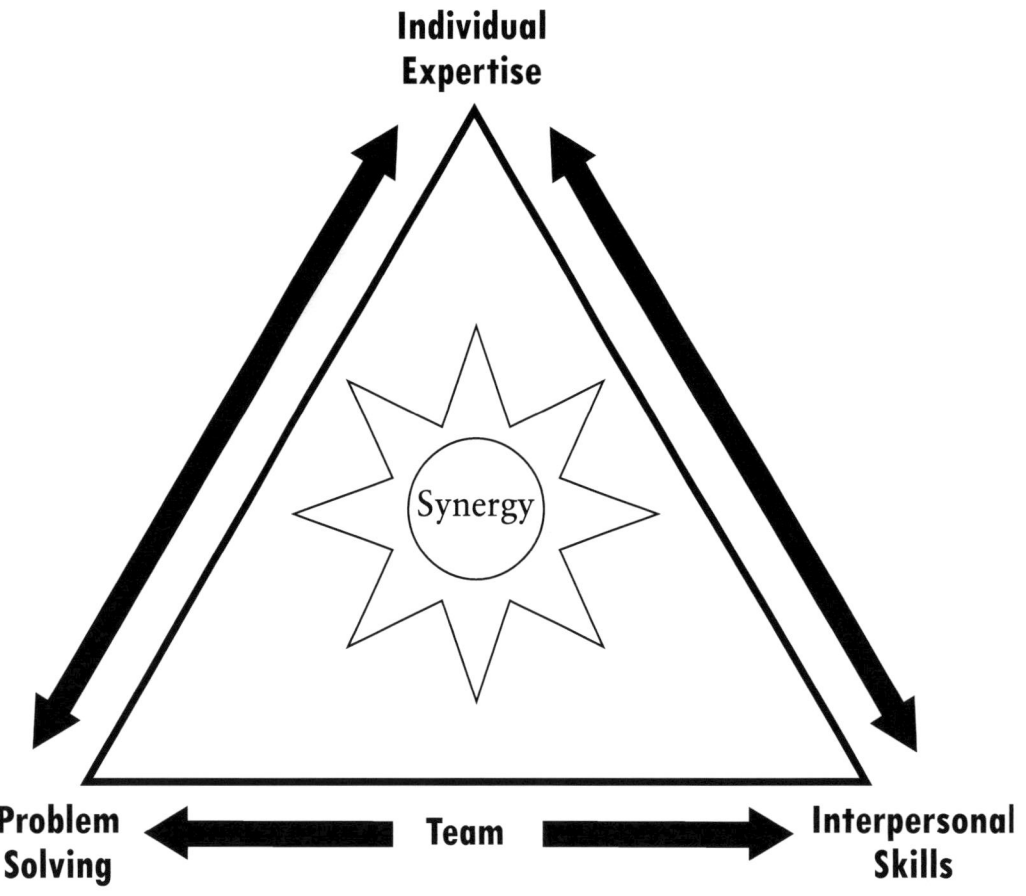

HOW EFFECTIVE IS OUR TEAM?

To determine how effectively your team worked together on this problem and whether the team reached synergy on its decisions, complete the steps below. You may also want to compare your team to other teams that have worked on this problem. Space is provided for entering the scores of up to five additional teams.

Step 1 **Average Individual Score** Add the Individual Total scores from the Scoring Chart for all of the members of your team and divide by the number of members.						
Step 2 **Team Score** Enter your Team Total score from the Scoring Chart.						
Step 3 **Difference Score** Subtract the Team Score from the Average Individual Score. If the Team Score is lower, put a (+) sign with the Difference Score. If the Average Individual Score is lower, put a (-) sign with the Difference Score.						
Step 4 **Team Effectiveness Score (%)** Divide the Difference Score by the Average Individual Score. The larger the percentage, the greater the team's effectiveness.						
Step 5 **Best Individual Score** Enter the best (lowest) Individual Total score here. This person was the team's best resource.						
Step 6 **Unused Team Resources** How many Individual Total scores were lower than the Team Score? This represents the resources that were not sufficiently utilized.						
Step 7 **Synergy** Was Synergy reached? Enter Yes or No. Synergy is achieved when the Team Score (Step 2) is lower (better) than the score achieved by the best individual resource on your team (Step 5).						

TEAM REFLECTION AND ACTION PLANNING

1. How did your team perform during the *Black Bear* activity? If you didn't achieve synergy, what behaviors (or lack of them) contributed to the end result?

2. How well does your team typically handle decision-making under pressure?

3. Which parts of the Effective Decision-Making Process does your team need to work on? How will you do that?

REFERENCES

Anderson, T. (1992). *Black Bear: Seasons in the Wild.* Stillwater, MN: Voyageur Press.

Angier, B. (1956). *How to Stay Alive in the Woods.* New York: Macmillan.

Appalachian Trail Guide to Tennessee-North Carolina (10th ed.). (1992). Harpers Ferry, WV: Appalachian Trail Conference.

Auerbach & Geehr. (1988). *Management of Wilderness and Environmental Emergencies.* St. Louis, MO: Mosby-Yearbook.

Bruce, D. (1991). *The Thru-hiker's Handbook.* Harpers Ferry, WV: Appalachian Trail Conference.

Fair, J. (1990). *The Great American Bear.* Minocqua, WI: NorthWord Press.

Herrero, S. (1985). *Bear Attacks.* New York: Lyons & Burford.

Lentz, M., Macdonald, S., & Carline, J. (1985). *Mountaineering First Aid.* Seattle, WA: The Mountaineers.

Tilton, B. (1990). *The Basic Essentials of Rescue from the Backcountry.* Merrillville, IN: ICS Books.

Tilton, B., & Hubbell, F. (1990). *Medicine for the Backcountry.* Merrillville, IN: ICS Books.

Janis, I. L. (1989). *Crucial Decisions.* New York: The Free Press.

Pinsdorf, M. K. (1987). *Communicating When Your Company is Under Siege.* Lexington, MA: Lexington Books.

Reilly, A. H. (1987). Are organizations ready for crisis? A managerial scorecard. *Columbia Journal of World Business, 23,* 79-88.

Stubbart, C. I. (1987). Improving the quality of crisis thinking. *Columbia Journal of World Business, 23,* 89-99.

About the Expert

Buck Tilton is director of the Wilderness Medicine Institute, Inc., in Pitkin, Colorado; co-author of *Medicine for the Backcountry*; author of *The Basic Essentials of Rescue from the Backcountry*, *The Basic Essentials of Avalanche Safety*, and many magazine articles on wilderness medicine and rescue; member of the Outdoor Writers Association of America; and a member of the American Medical Writers Association.

About the HRDQ Research and Development Team

HRDQ's commitment to theory-driven products and services starts with our Research & Development Team. Our development process is the backbone of all of our products and services, whether we're creating off-the-shelf learning instruments or custom interventions. In addition to holding advanced degrees, all of our team members are trained in behavioral science research techniques and have practical training-room experience, so you can be assured that the products you are purchasing have been professionally developed and scientifically tested.

For more information about the HRDQ Research & Development Team,
please visit our website at www.hrdq.com

About This Product

Developer Bradford R. Glaser

Bradford R. Glaser is president of HRDQ. He has been with HRDQ since 1989 and has held numerous positions in marketing, sales, and management. He holds a B.A. from Clark University in Worcester, MA. In 1992, Brad successfully thru-hiked the Appalachian Trail, beginning on Springer Mountain in Georgia on April 7th and finishing on Mount Katahdin in Maine on October 8th.

Special thanks to my family and all my A.T. friends who made my thru-hike complete: Mom, Dad, Jim and Barbara Roadcap, Debbie "Pacer" Clinard, David "Kunning Kat" Cunningham, Steven "Wayward Son" Dorio and Jesse "Sidekick" the dog, Suzy "Pooh" Foreman, Kurt "Tortilla" Grossman, Curtis "Cool Breeze" Haley, Ken "Young Gun" Jensen, Dave "Source" McCarriar, Mike "Cruz Control" McDonnell, Chris "Nomadman" Nottoli, and Carmen "Firefly" and Frank "Slow-to-Go" Patterson.

About HRDQ

HRDQ is a leader in the development of experiential learning solutions that improve the performance of individuals, teams, and organizations. Our capabilities include a wide range of programs, assessments, games, activities, and simulations that address the challenges of today's business community, from coaching and communication, to team building, leadership, and more.